Steve Tash

Gilead Books Publishing

www.GileadBooksPublishing.com

First published in Great Britain September 2020

2 4 6 8 10 9 7 5 3 1

Copyright ©Stephen Tash 2020

British Library Cataloguing-in-Publication Data:

A catalogue record for this book is available from the British Library.

ISBN: 978-1-9997224-9-4

All rights reserved.

No part of this publication may be reproduced, stored in a retrieval system or transmitted in any form or by any means, electronic, mechanical, photocopying, recording or otherwise, without the prior permission of the publisher.

All scripture quotations, unless otherwise indicated, are taken from the HOLY BIBLE, NEW INTERNATIONAL VERSION. Copyright © 1973, 1978, 1984 by International Bible Society. Used by permission of Hodder & Stoughton, a member of the Hodder Headline Group. All rights reserved. 'NIV' is a trademark of International Bible Society. UK trademark number 1448790.

Scripture quotations marked (ESV) are from The ESV® Bible (The Holy Bible, English Standard Version®), copyright © 2001 by Crossway, a publishing ministry of Good News Publishers. Used by permission. All rights reserved.

Cover image ©Anna Tash

To all those who care for us, thank you.

'…weep with those who weep.'
(Romans 12:15 ESV)

Contents

Introduction	7
It's all about love	9
Downcast and disturbed	10
He set my feet on a rock	12
Jesus	13
Joy in your presence	14
Jesus at creation	16
Light again	17
Light in the dark	18
Astonished	20
King of Creation	23
Trust when you cannot trust	27
New	29
Holy Communion	30
Bread and Wine	32
Crucifixion	34
Abandonment	37
Forgive	39
He died, but he rose again	41
Women witnesses	44
The road to Emmaus	46
New life for us	50
Pentecost	51
Our seasons	53
Everything comes right in the end, but where did it all go wrong?	55
Through a glass	58
I am making everything new!	60
Fear	63
Sleep has gone	64
Consumed by regret	66
Physical health	68
Parents	70
Do not harm yourself	72
A Saviour	76
A final thought—is there any meaning in my suffering?	78

Foreword

This is a book, full of compassion and wisdom, for those struggling with mental health. It is also an introduction to the Christian faith. The author has himself experienced times of deep darkness and struggle in his own life, which gives the writing an authenticity and a gentle conviction. Today, thank God, mental illness is coming out of the closet of shame and is recognised as something many, if not most of us, will experience at some stage in our life. This book is both timely and deeply human, the work of a wounded healer who has faith in the one by whose wounds we are healed. (Isaiah 53:5) Suffused with Christian love for those in a place of darkness and struggle, it offers both hope and solidarity. It is enhanced by the fine drawings of the author's daughter, Anna.

The Rt Revd John Stroyan
Bishop of Warwick

Acknowledgements

When this project began few of us had heard of coronavirus or Zoom. These two people who work in healthcare have therefore been stretched. Many thanks to Chris for your publishing work, your excellent formatting and suggestions, especially during such testing times.

Thank you, Anna, for your deep well of encouragement, your suggestions and for using one of your many gifts in this book.

Thank you, Julia, for unbelievably observant proofreading.

Thank you to patients who have allowed me to share in your lives. Thank you to staff in the hospitals who have been both colleagues and companions. You have all taught me so much.

Introduction

There are times when many of us suffer illness in our minds. Our poorly brains are not working as they should. I have known such times myself. I had a very serious bout of mental illness which lasted some three years. I know of the medication so many of us take and the hours spent in bed since getting up to wash and dress seem like massive tasks. Jobs are lost; reputations changed; money becomes a problem; homes can be lost too. Mental illness can change everything for those of us who suffer it and it can take a very large toll on those who care for us.

The following Bible readings are especially for those of us who know what struggling with mental health is like.

They are mostly short because it may be hard to concentrate at the moment. But these readings speak of Jesus, the one who was God come to earth. There is love, light and there is hope.

I work as a chaplain in several mental health hospitals. On many occasions I am asked for a Bible. When I give one to somebody, I have wondered whether an accompanying book of readings like this one might help someone navigate its pages and be an introduction to Christian faith.

I am Anna's father and she is the artist behind the drawings. She too works in a caring profession and deeply wants those she nurses to know love and wholeness.

You may be so deep in depression that you won't get past this paragraph. Words are not going in through the barrier of illness. Nothing seems to help or touch us emotionally. But we hope you like the drawings. They are about growth, hope, light and life. It might be worth simply gazing on one drawing for some time. God's Spirit might help you as you look, wonder and think.

Perhaps you can come back and read the words when you feel better.

Steve Tash

It's all about love

Here are three words from the Bible as the first reading. They come from a letter called 1 John.

God is love

When we discover God we find love. The Bible is so filled with God's love. Becoming a Christian is all about love. As we read the Bible, we are reading about a God of love who loves us and the world he made. A very loving parent goes through many emotions with their children. There will be wonderfully happy times filled with joy, delight, tenderness, compassion and deep affection. But there will also be pain, grief, sadness, anger and frustration. Loving anyone deeply comes with the expectation of all these emotions and more.

So it is with God in the pages of the Bible which cover several thousand years of his dealings with humanity. But underpinning all these emotions we find the God of love, steadfast, pure, all embracing love. We who worship God are safe in his love.

> Lord, please reveal yourself and your love to me. Thank you.

DOWNCAST AND DISTURBED

How do we read anything when our minds are ill? It seems nothing goes in, we can't concentrate for long. Sorry that you are ill at the moment. I pray this gentle guide through the Bible will lead you towards the God who is love and where there is peace and healing.

Read Psalm 42 and verse 11. The Psalms are near the middle of the Bible.

> *Why are you downcast, O my soul? Why so disturbed within me?*
>
> *Put your hope in God, for I will yet praise him, my Saviour and my God.*

The Bible is a huge collection of 66 different books covering several thousand years. 'The Bible' means 'The Books.' It is a library of books. Today's verses from perhaps 3000 years ago, show that people have known for a long time what it is like to be downcast and disturbed. The answer was to put your hope in God. That is not easy when we feel no hope at all. Do you know any old hymns or songs? Is it worth singing one now to yourself even though you don't feel like it?

On YouTube you will find the lovely song, *As the Deer Longs for the Water*. This comes from the first verse of today's psalm.

You will find a lot of Christian music on YouTube, both old hymns and new songs. Listening to music can be a comfort.

Lord, please help me trust again.

HE SET MY FEET ON A ROCK

Another Psalm today. There are 150 Psalms in the Bible. Many of them were written by a King of Israel called David.

Read Psalm 40:1-2:

> *I waited patiently for the Lord; he turned to me and heard my cry.*
>
> *He lifted me out of the slimy pit, out of the mud and mire.*

In times of depression and darkness it is so hard to feel any inner light. We long for relief and can give up hope of it ever arriving. Here King David, after waiting patiently, senses he was in a pit that felt like slimy mud and mire. But God lifted him out and gave him something firm to stand on again, a rock. If you feel in a pit I hope it begins to allow some light in today.

Lord, please lift me out of this pit of illness.

JESUS

Jesus is the central character in the Bible. It all points towards him. It may feel odd beginning to read the Bible two thirds of the way through, but the life of Jesus is the place to start. Then it all makes sense.

Read the Gospel of John chapter 8 verse 12:

> *When Jesus spoke again to the people, he said, 'I am the light of the world. Whoever follows me will never walk in darkness, but will have the light of life.'*

In despair and darkness we need hope and light. Jesus claims to be the Light of the World and offers the light of life to his followers. That is some claim. Millions of people alive today believe it is true.

> Lord, please shine light on me.

JOY IN YOUR PRESENCE

Back to the Psalms.

Read Psalm 16 verse 11:

> *You have made known to me the path of life;*
>
> *You will fill me with joy in your presence, with eternal pleasures at your right hand.*

I expect some words have disappeared from your conversation at the moment. Words like, 'enjoy' or 'I am looking forward to.' In deep depression there can be little sense of happiness. Perhaps there are one or two people who you like being around, even at the moment, one or two who do bring a measure of comfort just by being alongside you.

Even though you may not 'feel' God's presence, this verse suggests that just being with him is 'joy'. Joy is not the same as happiness. Joy is a deeper kind of comfort, like knowing someone is there. Unlike happiness, joy doesn't really change with what's going on. Joy is more like an everlasting gift of security. Jesus speaks of giving us a peace which this world cannot give. It's worth pausing over that and reminding ourselves that there is a love beyond this world and there is a peace which is deeper than the peace this world might give. Joy comes from somewhere else and I guess its roots are in heaven. Our own experience of the world might be encased in dark depression at the moment. But there is a loving presence who only has your good in mind. God is always there, even when we are unaware. If we awoke from a deep coma we might think no one had been there with us. But a very loving friend who never left our bedside might say, 'I never left you. I was always there with you.'

Search for and read the lovely poem called *Footprints*.

> Lord, please be with me so I can sense joy.

JESUS AT CREATION

Christians worship Jesus as God; God come to earth.

There was a group of Christians in Colossae, an ancient town of modern Turkey. Paul, a Jewish leader who had encountered Jesus and had been converted to follow him, wrote to them.

Read Colossians chapter 1, verses 15-17:

> *He is the image of the invisible God, the firstborn over all creation. For by him all things were created: things in heaven and on earth, visible and invisible, whether thrones or powers or rulers or authorities; all things were created by him and for him. He is before all things, and in him all things hold together.*

God is invisible, Jesus was visible. People lived with him, ate with him, walked with him, talked with him. Some say, 'We can't see God.' But God became visible in Jesus. These verses suggest Jesus is the same God who created everything. What came before that Big Bang? Jesus was before all things.

Thank you Jesus for being our creator God.

LIGHT AGAIN

There was also a group of Christians in Corinth, in Greece. Paul wrote letters to them too.

Read a verse from 2 Corinthians chapter 4, verse 6:

For God, who said, 'Let light shine out of darkness,' made his light shine in our hearts to give us the light of the knowledge of the glory of God in the face of Christ.

This speaks of light too. In the first book of the Bible, Genesis, verse 3, God said, 'Let there be light.' God saw that the light was good. Paul, in this letter, reminds people that his light now shines in our hearts and we know the glory of God in the face of Christ. If we see Jesus, we see the glory of God. His good light can come to us in whatever situation we find ourselves in.

When the darkness of depression surrounds us and nothing seems to break through, ask for the light of God to be present, shining in the dark. It is good.

YouTube—*The Lord is my light, my light and salvation.* A chant from the Taizé community in France.

> Lord, thank you for being The Light of the World. Please shine in my dark.

LIGHT IN THE DARK

Read Psalm 18, verses 4-6 and 28:

> *The cords of death entangled me; the torrents of destruction overwhelmed me.*
>
> *The cords of the grave coiled around me; the snares of death confronted me.*
>
> *In my distress I called to the Lord; I cried to my God for help. From his temple he heard my voice; my cry came before him, into his ears...*
>
> *You, O Lord, keep my lamp burning; my God turns my darkness into light.*

A gentle 'well done' if you're still managing to read this. It is so hard to keep going in depression. Even putting one foot in front of the other can seem too much. It is tempting to want to curl up somewhere and be finished with everything. Despite David, who wrote this, feeling close to death, he manages to find strength to keep going. Call out to the Lord yourself for him to keep your lamp burning and to turn your dark to light. Do you know the old song that we often sang in schools? *Give me oil in my lamp keep me burning*—Try YouTube.

Lord, mostly I feel like giving up. Please keep me going and shine some light into my dark. Thank you.

Astonished

Astonishment and amazement are often present when Jesus was involved. As God come to earth doing only what God can do, it is no wonder humans were amazed.

Read Luke chapter 5, verses 4-11:

> *When he had finished speaking, he said to Simon, 'Put out into deep water, and let down the nets for a catch.'*
>
> *Simon answered, 'Master, we've worked hard all night and haven't caught anything. But because you say so, I will let down the nets.'*
>
> *When they had done so, they caught such a large number of fish that their nets began to break. So they signalled their partners in the other boat to come and help them, and they came and filled both boats so full that they began to sink.*
>
> *When Simon Peter saw this, he fell at Jesus' knees and said, 'Go away from me, Lord; I am a sinful man!' For he and all his companions were astonished at the catch of fish they had taken, and so were James and John, the sons of Zebedee, Simon's partners.*

> *Then Jesus said to Simon, 'Don't be afraid; from now on you will catch men.' So they pulled their boats up on shore, left everything and followed him.*

This is a short story of Jesus calling people to follow him. We don't use that word 'astonish' too much. It has to be something really surprising, like an *astonishing* world record long jump or an *astonishing* story of survival. It is often used for something superhuman. And that's the point, Jesus did superhuman things. He lived fully as a human, yet he was also fully God. Astonishing! See verse 9:

> *For he and all his companions were astonished at the catch of fish they had taken.*

One thought—if the story of Jesus was made up, there wouldn't be quite so many astonishing events. A writer of fiction would be overplaying his hand. Too many astonishing things and it becomes unbelievable, on a level with a fantasy like Superman or Wonder Woman.

Yet here in ancient Palestine is a man, so like others in most respects, eating, sleeping, the eldest child in a family, but also completely astonishing.

Thank you Lord that in your life we see
heaven come to earth in miraculous ways.
Please bring a touch of heaven to me today.
Thank you.

KING OF CREATION

There are four accounts of the life of Jesus at the beginning of the New Testament part of the Bible. These are Matthew, Mark, Luke and John. These were written down to record the unique life of someone like no other. The events which are written explain why we celebrate Christmas and Easter. These accounts also contain the priceless teaching and the miraculous signs Jesus did as he showed his love and his power.

Read John chapter 6, verses 5-13 and 16-21. You may have heard of these stories before, but they are gripping:

> *When Jesus looked up and saw a great crowd coming towards him, he said to Philip, 'Where shall we buy bread for these people to eat?' He asked this only to test him, for he already had in mind what he was going to do.*
>
> *Philip answered him, 'Eight months' wages would not buy enough bread for each one to have a bite!'*
>
> *Another of his disciples, Andrew, Simon Peter's brother, spoke up, 'Here is a boy with five small*

barley loaves and two small fish, but how far will they go among so many?'

Jesus said, 'Make the people sit down.' There was plenty of grass in that place, and the men sat down, about five thousand of them. Jesus then took the loaves, gave thanks, and distributed to those who were seated as much as they wanted. He did the same with the fish.

When they had all had enough to eat, he said to his disciples, 'Gather the pieces that are left over. Let nothing be wasted.' So they gathered them and filled twelve baskets with the pieces of the five barley loaves left over by those who had eaten.

When evening came, his disciples went down to the lake, where they got into a boat and set off across the lake for Capernaum. By now it was dark, and Jesus had not yet joined them. A strong wind was blowing and the waters grew rough. When they had rowed three or three and a half miles, they saw Jesus approaching the boat, walking on the water; and they were terrified. But he said to them, 'It is I; don't be afraid.' Then they were willing to take him into the boat, and immediately the boat reached the shore where they were heading.

Only someone who created bread and fish and sea could use them in this way. The Bible speaks of a King of Creation and surely Jesus embodies him.

Jesus' miracles were very deep and powerful signs of his compassion and of his identity. People who were blind, deaf and lame are healed. There are moving accounts of dead people being raised again to life with all of the accompanying awe and joy for those bereaved. The Gospel of John speaks of these as signs of who Jesus was and they are written down so his readers might believe.

As we read through the history of the Jewish faith in the Old Testament, we see similar miracles occurring, especially those performed by the prophets Elijah and Elisha. It seems that the same God of love was expressing deep and powerful compassion in the Old Testament as Jesus did in the New Testament. It is the same God at work.

If God can make and remake, think of how he can use your life and what he can make of it. People inspired by their faith have done truly remarkable things. Think of Wilberforce abolishing slavery, or Cicely Saunders founding the hospice movement, or Martin Luther King championing civil rights in America. In recent times we can think of Chad Varah who set up Samaritans. God has done wonderful things through those who serve him. What can he do through you?

> Lord, thank you for your love and power.
> Please use me, please make something of
> my life.

TRUST WHEN YOU CANNOT TRUST

Read Proverbs, near the centre of the Bible, chapter 3 verse 5:

> *Trust in the Lord with all your heart and lean not on your own understanding;*
>
> *in all your ways acknowledge him, and he will make your paths straight.*

Proverbs is a fascinating book of sayings. Many verses feel self-contained and can be real gems. The book encourages wisdom. It's a lovely book to browse around.

The verse today encourages us to trust in the Lord with all our heart, even with the broken bits. But how to trust when the illness goes on and on, when prayers seems to go nowhere, when God may feel miles away. There is so much we don't understand. We don't have answers to everything. But there is enough we do understand and there is enough order in the world to show us that it isn't chaos.

There are more people out of hospitals than in hospitals. There are a million acts of kindness being done at this very moment to far outweigh the awful news on TV. So we trust in God for the things we can make sense of and the things we can't.

> Lord, there are many things I do not understand, like my own illness. But I choose to trust you with my sad and broken heart anyway.

New

The old has gone, the new has come. This is a central message of the Bible.

Read 2 Corinthians chapter 5, verse 17:

> *Therefore, if anyone is in Christ, he is a new creation; the old has gone, the new has come!*

We are reading Paul's second letter to the Christians in Corinth, Greece. God is making everything new. Jesus, when he rose from the grave, is the firstborn in a new creation. All things are being made new, the old has gone, the new has come. We will read later how God is making a new heaven and a new earth. Now, if we follow Jesus as our king, he makes us new. Paul uses the phrase 'in Christ' to describe those early Christians.

> Lord, may I be in Christ. Please make me new.

HOLY COMMUNION

Read Matthew chapter 26, verses 26-28:

> *While they were eating, Jesus took bread, gave thanks and broke it, and gave it to his disciples, saying, 'Take and eat; this is my body.'*
>
> *Then he took the cup, gave thanks and offered it to them, saying, 'Drink from it, all of you. This is my blood of the covenant, which is poured out for the many for the forgiveness of sins.'*

Churches have remembered and celebrated this meal for some 2000 years. There are many understandings of it and many names for it like: Mass, The Lord's Supper, Eucharist (which is Greek for thanksgiving) Holy Communion and so on.

My mind wasn't working well, so thinking about faith was hard. I did though manage to take Holy Communion occasionally. I could join in the meal that Jesus told us to remember. I could eat bread and drink wine. The words sometimes said at a Holy Communion service are, 'Feed on him in your hearts.' Ideas about faith appeal to our minds. But this bread and wine are touched, tasted and taken in to our hearts. We feed on

Jesus in our hearts, even when our minds are not working well.

When our minds are poorly it is useful to use other senses to help our faith. I kept a postcard in my pocket of a painting called 'Jesus the Light of the World'. Touching that postcard was like touching my faith, because I couldn't connect with God with my mind. We may never fully understand the depths of the meal Jesus told us to remember, and sometimes our minds are too ill to understand anyway. But we can eat and drink.

> Thank you Lord for bread to eat and wine to drink in remembrance of you.

Bread and Wine

Read Luke chapter 22, verses 19-20:

> *And he took bread, gave thanks and broke it, and gave it to them, saying, 'This is my body given for you; do this in remembrance of me.'*
>
> *In the same way, after the supper he took the cup, saying, 'This cup is the new covenant in my blood, which is poured out for you.'*

It was hard for the first followers of Jesus to understand the meal. Jesus said, 'This is my body given for you,' and, 'This cup is the new covenant in my blood, which is poured out for you.' What did he mean? It must have sounded confusing. But when they saw him dying on the cross, his body failing and his blood flowing, they must have made a connection with the words at the meal. The bread and the wine make us think of the cross where Jesus hung and died. So the meal reminds us of his deep and sacrificial love. It reminds us that he gave everything to rescue us from sin and death. Rescuing us must have been very important, given the agonising lengths God went to.

Lord, "Love so amazing, so divine, demands my soul, my life, my all." As you gave yourself for me, I gladly give myself to you. Take me and use me in your service.

Crucifixion

Read Mark chapter 15, verses 22-32:

> They brought Jesus to the place called Golgotha (which means The Place of the Skull). Then they offered him wine mixed with myrrh, but he did not take it. And they crucified him. Dividing up his clothes, they cast lots to see what each would get.
>
> It was the third hour when they crucified him. The written notice of the charge against him read: THE KING OF THE JEWS. They crucified two robbers with him, one on his right and one on his left. Those who passed by hurled insults at him, shaking their heads and saying, 'So! You who are going to destroy the temple and build it in three days, come down from the cross and save yourself!'
>
> In the same way the chief priests and the teachers of the law mocked him among themselves. 'He saved others,' they said, 'but he can't save himself! Let this Christ, this King of Israel, come down from the cross, that we may see and believe.' Those crucified with him also heaped insults on him.

It seems truly dreadful that someone as loving and compassionate as Jesus should be executed in this barbaric way. He had performed such wonders and healed so many. His teaching was so wise and appealing. The religious leaders of his day couldn't make him out. Only 33 years old, this Jesus was attracting great crowds and interpreting their religion differently. He seemed more concerned with compassion in action than keeping strict religious rules. He was claiming God's authority for what he was doing and, in the eyes of the religious leaders, was speaking blasphemy. Despite all the wonders, the goodness, the transformed healed lives which followed in the wake of wherever Jesus went, the religious leaders didn't get it. They were jealous, indignant and outraged. They managed to persuade the occupying Roman authorities to do away with him.

> Lord, never let me be blinded to your love
> and goodness.

ABANDONMENT

Read Mark chapter 15, verses 33-34 and 37:

> *At the sixth hour darkness came over the whole land until the ninth hour. And at the ninth hour Jesus cried out in a loud voice, 'Eloi, Eloi, lama sabachthani?'—which means, 'My God, my God, why have you forsaken me?'*
>
> *With a loud cry, Jesus breathed his last.*

Jesus cries out, 'My God, my God, why have you forsaken me?'

These are dreadful cries of sadness, pain and despair. Jesus cries out, God where are you? Why have you forgotten me?

I am reminded how, in depression, God can seem absent. It is almost as if a part of our mind, the part which is about faith, has closed off and isn't working. If it were a physical sensation then we might say our sense of touch had gone. But in our minds it is as if faith has gone, God has gone.

I find it so reassuring that Jesus, in some way, experienced this sense of abandonment from God. How dreadful this must have been for God the Son to lose a sense of God the Father. God has lost something of who he is. For God to have put himself through such an appalling ordeal there must have been a very large reason. And there is. God did this out of love for you and me to put us right with him.

> Lord, I feel abandoned by you at times.
> Thank you that Jesus felt this too. Keep my
> faith alive please Lord, especially when it
> feels that you have left me.

Forgive

Read Luke chapter 23, verses 32-34:

> *Two other men, both criminals, were also led out to be executed. When they came to the place called The Skull, there they crucified him, along with the criminals - one on his right and one on his left. Jesus said, 'Father forgive them, for they do not know what they are doing.' And they divided up his clothes by casting lots.*

Jesus prays that those executing him will be forgiven, for they don't know what they are doing. He is extraordinary. It is a wonder that as he experiences terrible pain he wants to forgive those causing it.

The cross is where we can all find God's forgiveness. Sometimes we judge ourselves harshly. Sometimes we cannot forgive ourselves. We feel so guilty. In mental illness the weight of our conscience can be unbearable. The guilt feels so heavy.

But in the end, who are we to judge anyone? Who are we even to judge ourselves? Only a perfect judge can judge perfectly and that is God. At the cross of Jesus, God forgives. The heavenly judge cancels our sin.

Now think about it hard. If God, the only one qualified to judge perfectly, does not condemn us, why should we condemn ourselves? Are we better judges than God?

If we seek his forgiveness, it is there for us. An old hymn says, *'My chains fell off, my heart was free, I rose went forth and followed thee.'*

> Lord, I am so sorry for so many things, please forgive me.

He died, but he rose again

Read John chapter 20, verses 14-16:

> *At this, she turned around and saw Jesus standing there, but she did not realise that it was Jesus.*
>
> *'Woman,' he said, 'why are you crying? Who is it you are looking for?'*
>
> *Thinking he was the gardener, she said, 'Sir, if you have carried him away, tell me where you have put him, and I will get him.'*
>
> *Jesus said to her, 'Mary.'*

Jesus died on Friday. The event described here happens early on Sunday. Mary Magdalene went to the tomb and found that the stone at the tomb's entrance had been removed. She then ran to tell the others who also ran to the tomb to see. After they had gone Mary stayed there. She was crying when remarkable and unexpected things began to happen.

This account in John chapter 20 is wonderful. It has been read around fires at dawn in many church gardens and the like. As the light comes up on Easter Day, some Christians take a new light on a taper out of the fire and light candles with it. Sometimes a very large candle is lit and taken into a church where there is singing and celebration. It is to recall what is arguably the greatest historical event. Jesus was dead, but is alive again. After rising to life again, he insists that he isn't a ghost. He invites folk to touch him and he eats with them. He says he has flesh and bones.

Yes, it is remarkable. If Jesus had not come alive again it is probably certain that we would never have heard about him. He was a young man in the Middle East a couple of thousand years ago, he did and said things which caused a local stir for about three years. This was a pinhead moment in the vast stretch of history.

Yet, because he overcame death, his place in history is at the top of the list. People now wrote down about his life, his miracles and his teaching. Now they were certain God had walked amongst them in the person of Jesus. Now they worshipped him. The writings in the New Testament are working out the deep meaning of Jesus' life, his death and his resurrection. Someone, like no one before or since has lived, died and been seen alive again. Jesus is unique. What can it all mean for the world?

The fact that we have even heard about Jesus shows that something out of this world happened on that first Easter Sunday. His resurrection is more than a coming alive again. Jesus did not come back to life as someone who would one day die again. No, Jesus was now alive as someone who had overcome death. His was a resurrection, not a resuscitation. He is the model now of a new humanity, the one to which we join as we follow him.

The risen Jesus turns to Mary and says her name. Imagine him saying your name.

> Thank you Lord for your power over death.
> Help me understand what this means for me.

WOMEN WITNESSES

Read Luke chapter 24, verses 10-12:

> *It was Mary Magdalene, Joanna, Mary the mother of James, and the others with them who told this to the apostles. But they did not believe the women, because their words seemed to them like nonsense. Peter, however, got up and ran to the tomb. Bending over, he saw the strips of linen lying by themselves, and he went away, wondering to himself what had happened.*

Women went to Jesus' tomb with spices they had prepared. Saturday was their Sabbath when they couldn't visit, but now they could. They saw and heard extraordinary things there and in this reading they have returned to tell the men.

Luke was a doctor who researched accounts about Jesus before writing his own. Eyewitnesses all see something different. Their different perspectives give history the ring of truth. Luke writes about women telling the men what they had seen at Jesus' tomb on the Sunday morning. This is a little different from what

John writes but, as I say, this gives history the ring of truth.

If they had made up the accounts it is extremely unlikely they would have used women as their eyewitnesses. The place of women in those days was not recognised. They were undervalued. No writer then would have used women for such a prominent role if it hadn't actually happened that way. But these writers are not making it up. So they tell it like it was. Women were the first eyewitnesses of Jesus rising to life again.

> Thank you Lord, that you are alive and here with me now. Thank you that you treat women and men equally.

The Road to Emmaus

Read Luke chapter 24, verses 13-35:

This is a lovely story and is often read on the evening of Easter Day.

> *Now that same day two of them were going to a village called Emmaus, about seven miles from Jerusalem. They were talking with each other about everything that had happened. As they talked and discussed these things with each other, Jesus himself came up and walked along with them; but they were kept from recognising him.*
>
> *He asked them, 'What are you discussing together as you walk along?'*
>
> *They stood still; their faces downcast. One of them, named Cleopas, asked him, 'Are you the only one living in Jerusalem who doesn't know the things that have happened there in these days?'*
>
> *'What things?' he asked.*
>
> *'About Jesus of Nazareth,' they replied. 'He was a prophet, powerful in word and deed before God and all the people. The chief priests and our rulers*

handed him over to be sentenced to death, and they crucified him; but we had hoped that he was the one who was going to redeem Israel. And what is more, it is the third day since all this took place. In addition, some of our women amazed us. They went to the tomb early this morning but didn't find his body. They came and told us that they had seen a vision of angels, who said he was alive. Then some of our companions went to the tomb and found it just as the women had said, but him they did not see.'

He said to them, 'How foolish you are, and how slow of heart to believe all that the prophets have spoken! Did not the Christ have to suffer these things and then enter his glory?' And beginning with Moses and all the Prophets, he explained to them what was said in all the Scriptures concerning himself.

As they approached the village to which they were going, Jesus acted as if he were going further. But they urged him strongly, 'Stay with us, for it is nearly evening; the day is almost over.' So he went in to stay with them.

> *When he was at the table with them, he took bread, gave thanks, broke it and began to give it to them. Then their eyes were opened and they recognised him, and he disappeared from their sight. They asked each other, 'Were not our hearts burning within us while he talked with us on the road and opened the Scriptures to us?'*
>
> *They got up and returned at once to Jerusalem. There they found the Eleven and those with them, assembled together and saying, 'It is true! The Lord has risen and has appeared to Simon.' Then the two told what had happened on the way, and how Jesus was recognised by them when he broke the bread.*

This is a remarkable story. Were they two men walking together to Emmaus? Were they a married couple? We cannot be sure. They were having a pretty strong discussion. The Greek word used in the Bible suggests it could have been an argument. For most of this journey they don't recognise Jesus. I wonder why? He tells them where in the Old Testament it points to him. Their hearts were burning with such a brilliant Bible study! When they do recognise him, he disappears.

On our life's journey there are times when we feel close to God and times we don't. But we always have the Bible to remind us of the truth of who Jesus is.

> Thank you Lord that we find you in the Old Testament as well as in the New Testament. Thank you for your resurrection.

NEW LIFE FOR US

Read Romans chapter 6, verses 4-5:

> *We were therefore buried with him through baptism into death in order that, just as Christ was raised from the dead through the glory of the Father, we too may live a new life.*
>
> *If we have been united with him in his death, we will certainly also be united with him in his resurrection.*

This is a letter to the church in Rome. Paul wrote it. He actually died in Rome too we think.

We can start again. All that has been spoiled in this life can be remade and started afresh. Because Jesus was raised to life, so can we be, through faith in him. We can live a new life. And this new life goes on into eternity as even death cannot end it. Death didn't end it for Jesus and it doesn't end life for those 'in Christ.'

> Lord please give me this new life. I turn away from the old life of sin and toward the new life of Jesus.

Pentecost

Read Acts chapter 2, verses 1-4:

> *When the day of Pentecost came, they were all together in one place. Suddenly a sound like the blowing of a violent wind came from heaven and filled the whole house where they were sitting. They saw what seemed to be tongues of fire that separated and came to rest on each of them. All of them were filled with the Holy Spirit and began to speak in other tongues as the Spirit enabled them.*

When Jesus died he gave up his Spirit to God. In the book of Acts we read of his Spirit being poured out upon the first believers. They were filled with the Holy Spirit. This book is the second one written by Luke. It is about the Holy Spirit guiding and leading the first believers (who were not called Christians yet) into amazing acts of love, healing, giving and sharing. They were the first church. The day of Pentecost was a bit like a harvest festival. It was on this day that God poured his Spirit out upon those first believers. It is the birthday of the church. The church's role today is still to continue the work of Jesus enabled by his Spirit.

As we read on in this chapter there comes a strong sense of unity, as if God is binding people together in love. There were many foreigners visiting Jerusalem. Perhaps they had come to celebrate the Pentecost Festival. Yet as these people listen to the disciples from Galilee speaking about God's wonders, they hear them in their own languages. This really is awesome and seems to suggest that God was reaching out beyond one language to embrace the whole world in love. It is time for all peoples to hear about the God of love who has come in Jesus. In deed and in word, this is the church's role today.

> Lord, fill me with your Holy Spirit that I may live and love all people from all nations as you do.

OUR SEASONS

Read Psalm 74, verses 16-17:

The day is yours, and yours also the night; you established the sun and moon.

It was you who set all the boundaries of the earth; you made both summer and winter.

How hard it is in depression to notice anything. The seasons come and go. We may not even go outside. A snowdrop doesn't inspire us, we don't notice the colours of the leaves changing in autumn. We haven't the energy to join the children in making sandcastles in summer or snowmen in winter.

So we have to try. This psalm recognises the sun and the moon and says how God created seasons. This is a couple of thousand years before Galileo argued that the earth goes around the sun. We know now how seasons come and go. But the great scientist had real and devoted faith in God. There was no conflict in his mind between science and faith. We also know now how getting out in nature and appreciating its wonders is so good for our mental health. In the UK we are blessed with changing seasons. There is the warmth and fresh promise of Spring with so much new growth. Then, hopefully, some hot days when the shorts and tee shirts get an airing. Autumn arrives with glorious changing colours. Winter with its sharp crispness and every unique snowflake beautifying the mountains can be invigorating. Little wonder the old hymn, *All Things Bright and Beautiful*, is still so popular. Today, try and notice one thing and give thanks. Sing or hum a verse of the old hymn.

> Lord, thank you for the seasons. Help me today to notice something beautiful.

EVERYTHING COMES RIGHT IN THE END, BUT WHERE DID IT ALL GO WRONG?

Read Genesis chapter 3, verses 16-19:

> *To the woman he said, 'I will greatly increase your pains in childbearing; with pain you will give birth to children. Your desire will be for your husband, and he will rule over you.*
>
> *To Adam he said, 'Because you listened to your wife and ate from the tree about which I commanded you, 'You must not eat of it,'*
>
> *'Cursed is the ground because of you; through painful toil you will eat of it all the days of your life. It will produce thorns and thistles for you, and you will eat the plants of the field. By the sweat of your brow you will eat your food until you return to the ground, since from it you were taken; for dust you are and to dust you will return.'*

In Genesis, God made everything and it was good. We do need to remember that the earth is good, creation is good. It is often breathtakingly beautiful. And yet, and yet. You may feel so depressed that even though once you could look, appreciate, feel, and your senses were alive to beauty, now it all feels dull. Nothing seems to penetrate the screen of dullness, no feelings, no goodness, not even love.

This is illness. The awful illness which dulls our lives and our senses and makes nothing seem to matter anymore.

Yes, the world all went wrong. The account of Adam and Eve eating from the tree of the knowledge of good and evil is the Bible's description of how it all went wrong. Now Adam and Eve will die. Death arrives. (Genesis 2: 17) They disobeyed God. The consequences are listed and they sound so sad, 'for dust you are and to dust you will return.' They are banished from Eden. There is also a sense that men oppressing women came from all this. You may be interested in whether these ancient writings are history or allegory but the meaning is the important thing and the meaning is that humanity disobeyed God. There was a parting of the ways between God and humanity and the consequences are disastrous.

God is the creator of life. There is no life without God. If we live with him, we live. If we do not want him, we die. That seems to be the underlying message of Genesis 3.

And there follows the terrifying consequences of humanity living this gift of life in the wrong way. We decay and die. Our moral compass is skewed, people get hurt, our appetites for material wealth get skewed. We choose killing. Our lives decay into hatred, greed and lust. We don't judge justly. Our bodies decay into illness, mental and physical. Even the earth moves out of order and into chaos sometimes. If we'd only heeded God and recognised it was all a gift and stayed close to the giver of it all.

I know we are into deep philosophy here, but this is how the Bible describes the origins of our decay.

Thank God he puts it all right in the end.

> Lord, please forgive my part in making the world a sad place. I turn to you. Help me to work with you in putting things right.

THROUGH A GLASS

Read I Corinthians chapter 13, verses 12-13. This is quite a short chapter and a very well-known one. Do read it all if you have a Bible.

> *Now we see <u>but a poor reflection</u>; then we shall see face to face. Now I know in part; then I shall know fully, even as I am fully known.*
>
> *And now these three remain: faith, hope and love. But the greatest of these is love.*

This is often read at weddings as it is a beautiful piece about love. Remember the first reading in this book; it's all about love.

An older Bible translation (the Bible is mostly written in Hebrew and Greek so we have to translate it into English) does not say 'but a poor reflection,' (underlined above) but, 'through a glass, darkly.'

In depression we can have the experience of living as normal but as if we are behind a glass divide from reality. Everything is happening as usual and we are able to function, but we feel one step removed. Our minds have seemingly stopped engaging fully. It is hard to describe, but it is like being the other side of a glass partition to everything that is happening. It's remarkable how we can still function and people do not realise there is anything wrong.

In this beautiful chapter on love, Paul is writing that now we experience God as if looking through a glass, obscurely. But he looks to the 'then' when we see God face to face. One day, not only our illness is ended, but everything that obscures our vision of God will be removed. Imagine that day!

> Lord, it is hard to carry on behind this 'glass divide' of illness. Please give me strength to continue and please bring your healing.
> Thank you that the day is coming when I meet your love, face to face.

I AM MAKING EVERYTHING NEW!

Read Revelation chapter 21, verses 1-5:

> *Then I saw a new heaven and a new earth, for the first heaven and the first earth had passed away, and there was no longer any sea. I saw the Holy City, the new Jerusalem, coming down out of heaven from God, prepared as a bride beautifully dressed for her husband. And I heard a loud voice from the throne saying, 'Now the dwelling of God is with men, and he will live with them. They will be his people, and God himself will be with them and be their God. He will wipe away every tear from their eyes. There will be no more death or mourning or crying or pain, for the old order of things has passed away.'*
>
> *He who was seated on the throne said, 'I am making everything new!' Then he said, 'Write this down, for these words are trustworthy and true.*

This last book of the Bible ends with such hope. Here we see how God puts everything right. There is a new heaven and a new earth. God comes to live with humanity. It sounds like Eden, when God was close to Adam and Eve, before it all went wrong in the first book of the Bible. Now here, at the end, which is a new beginning, there is life with no tears, no death, no mourning, crying or pain. Everything is made new.

Somewhere deep within our hearts, haven't we always dreamt of an end to war, killing, hatred and injustice? Haven't we imagined a painless and peaceful world? Haven't we hoped that the awful and frightening death, which robs us of our loved ones, would be no more?

Here, near the very end of the Bible, we have the vision of it happening and that means there is meaning and there is hope. One day, God will put everything right. We come to see that what we imagined and longed for in our hearts, came from a deep place within, which knew the truth. Our inner hopes are not disappointed.

> Thank you Lord, that there is hope. Help me
> cling to it.

(Parts of Revelation are difficult to understand. Some people with mental health struggles can find some parts disturbing. If you do read more of Revelation, do ask for the help of a mature Christian who can guide you through.)

Fear

Read John chapter 14, verse 27:

> *Peace I leave with you; my peace I give you. I do not give to you as the world gives. Do not let your hearts be troubled and do not be afraid.*

Ask for Jesus' peace. It is a better peace than the world gives. He wants us to feel secure. He wants us to be free from fear. I see God as the most loving parent, arms wrapped around us in a love which accepts us, forgives us, makes us safe and makes us whole. Close your eyes, breathe deeply and hear God's words, "My peace I give you...do not be afraid." In all the fearful turmoil of a poorly mind try and sense God's still small voice saying words of love and affirmation.

Somehow love heals our fears.

> Lord, sometimes my fears and anxieties cripple me. They seem sometimes to overwhelm me. Please come to me with your peace. I need your love to calm the storms within.

SLEEP HAS GONE

Read some verses from Psalm 77:

> *I cried out to God for help; I cried out to God to hear me.*
>
> *When I was in distress, I sought the Lord; at night I stretched out untiring hands and my soul refused to be comforted.*
>
> *I remembered you, O God, and I groaned; I mused, and my spirit grew faint.*
>
> *You kept my eyes from closing; I was too troubled to speak.*

There seems no comfort at all. In sleepless distress and in groaning we toss and turn until the grey dawn tells us we haven't slept.

Later in this psalm, the writer thinks back to better times. Remembering better times can help. God has done great things in the Bible. He hasn't changed. It is our illness which makes us feel so wretched. God has been a shepherd, leading his people. He still leads us, even when we can't sleep and even when we are not able to be mindful of his love.

We are learning how important sleep is to our well-being. We are learning that we need to come off our screens well before sleep time. We need to create an atmosphere in the bedroom, perhaps dimming the lighting, to get ready for sleep. We need good regular sleep habits.

> Lord please help me to sleep. In the meantime, as I lie awake, help me to find out all the wonders you have done in the past and think about them.

Consumed by regret

Read Lamentations chapter 3, verses 19-23:

> *I remember my affliction and my wandering, the bitterness and the gall.*
>
> *I well remember them, and my soul is downcast within me.*
>
> *Yet this I call to mind and therefore I have hope:*
>
> *Because of the Lord's great love we are not consumed, for his compassions never fail. They are new every morning; great is your faithfulness.*

The 'What Ifs', feel unmanageable at times. The regrets are so heavy and they fix us to the spot or we cannot move out of the chair. We ruminate upon them endlessly and find movement almost impossible. We dwell on the past and long for a time-machine to take us back to a time before all this, perhaps to a time before a wrong decision or to a time before something dreadful happened.

In this reading the memories sound bitter, the affliction awful. The inner soul is so low, so downcast. But there is something to call to mind: The Lord's great love.

Because of God's love the sadness doesn't completely consume us. God's compassions are new every morning and he is faithful to us. There is a way out of the deep dark place and it is God's love. Even in the deepest darkness, a light is shining.

You are a hero for keeping going. Journeying through depression is one of the toughest and bravest of challenges. Keep on. Keep putting one foot in front of the other.

> Lord, when I am engulfed by heavy regret and stuck in my low mood, give me strength to keep going. I know that with your love and help I will not be consumed.

Physical Health

Read Psalm 73, verses 25-26:

> *Whom have I in heaven but you? And earth has nothing I desire besides you.*
>
> *My flesh and my heart may fail, but God is the strength of my heart and my portion forever.*

My flesh and my heart may fail. Indeed they will. We age, our bodies deteriorate. It is important in mental health to keep our physical health good and get checked regularly by doctors. Mental and physical health are related. We need enough sleep. We need to exercise. We need to eat the right kinds of foods and not overdo the sugar and salt. There are stories of people with severe mental health problems having physical causes. Someone with years of mental illness around eating, died. An autopsy revealed he had a conker stuck in his throat! Someone else wanted ECT because it helped with constipation! Staying physical healthy is a good way of staying mentally healthy.

But wonderfully, the psalm recognises that we are on the journey to glory. Our bodies and minds will indeed fail, hopefully after a full life, but God is the strength of our hearts and we will, as Psalm 23 puts it, 'dwell in the house of the Lord forever.'

> Lord, thank you for my health. Help me not
> to take it for granted and help me do what I
> can to stay healthy.

Parents

Read Psalm 27, verse 10:

Though my father and mother forsake me, the Lord will receive me.

The Lord can be the parent figure we may never have had. There are many who have lived in care homes for much of life. Some have never known a loving parent figure. For some their house was not a home, but a place of torment or abuse. How terribly sad that such a thing may have affected our mental health. We should have grown up full of loving nurture, making us whole on the inside so we could love ourselves and love others. But the opposite is true for many. Neglect, emotional and physical, has left us helpless, empty inside and hopeless.

But Scripture says that God loves us like a Mother and like a Father. Jesus called God 'Father' in a way no-one had ever done. It is no easy thing to begin to repair a self-image. But it can start here, with the knowledge that God loved us always, all along the years of abuse, and that he still loves us.

Lord, show me your love. Repair my low self-esteem. Bring me people who love me just as I am, like you do. Help me to find ways to love them too. I am empty, please fill me. I am low, please lift me up. I am dry, please give me living water. I think nothing of myself, please show me your thoughts about me. Please be my Mother and Father now.

Do not harm yourself

Read Acts chapter 16, verses 27-34:

Someone is about to kill himself, but thankfully discovers something new.

> *The jailer woke up, and when he saw the prison doors open, he drew his sword and was about to kill himself because he thought the prisoners had escaped. But Paul shouted, 'Don't harm yourself! We are all here!'*
>
> *The jailer called for lights, rushed in and fell trembling, before Paul and Silas. He then brought them out and asked, 'Sirs, what must I do to be saved?'*
>
> *They replied, 'Believe in the Lord Jesus, and you will be saved-you and your household.' Then they spoke the word of the Lord to him and to all the others in his house.*
>
> *At that hour of the night the jailer took them and washed their wounds: then immediately he and all his family were baptized. The jailer brought them into his house and set a meal before them; he was*

filled with joy because he had come to believe in God-he and his whole family.

You matter very much. Please keep going. You are deeply loved. Do not harm yourself. Please keep going. You can get better.

In this story Paul and Silas, the two missionaries, are in jail having been arrested because of their practice of their faith. They have been severely flogged. It looks like an act of God shakes open all the prison doors and the jailer is so afraid of the consequences that he is about to kill himself. His fear and desperation are overwhelming him. But there is a happy ending and his mood actually turns to joy in this story.

Fear and desperation. Many of us know what that is like. We wish to finish it, to end it all, to crawl under a bush and be left to die. We may be hurting ourselves, cutting ourselves, starving ourselves. We cannot face the pain of continuing. We hit our heads against a wall. We attempt to die. The cutting seems to help for a short while. So sadly we do it again and it gets worse.

But during this time our minds might not be working well at all. Everything has possibly gone negative and hopeless. We don't even think about those left behind. We just may not be thinking straight. We need to wait for our minds to get better and we will see things differently.

Hear the shout of this verse, 'Don't harm yourself!' Things were not as bad as they seemed for this man and things may not be as bad as our minds are telling us at the moment. Keep going and get well. Things will seem different then.

This jailer person found joy when he came to believe in God. We can get better after terrible times of illness. There is a person in the Old Testament who suffers so much. His name is Job. The book of Job looks at the tough questions surrounding faith and suffering. Job, having gone through so much, finds great blessing later in his life.

The Bible says that God's love is steadfast. When all is changing, his love remains. You matter so much to God although at the moment that is difficult to believe. But you really do matter.

Keep going, keep trusting. Try very hard to wait patiently for healing.

Look at the app #StayAlive

Use SHOUT to text for help. It's a free texting support service. ***Text Shout to 85258***

For more information visit www.giveusashout.org.

Remember the Samaritans too. There are heart-warming stories of Chad Varah, the Anglican priest who started Samaritans in 1953. They now have 20,000 volunteers.

Perhaps with our experience of suffering mental ill health we might be able to understand and help fellow sufferers.

> Lord, all I want to do is end it all and I keep harming myself. Give me strength to overcome all this and keep going. Thank you that I matter very much to you.

A Saviour

Read Luke chapter 2 verse 11:

Today in the town of David a Saviour has been born to you; he is Christ the Lord.

There are many great titles for Jesus like, King, Lord, Good Shepherd, Light of the World. There is also 'Saviour.' Luke chapter 2 tells the wonderful Christmas story and you may recognise much of it.

A goalkeeper saves shots and penalties. A lifeboat crew saves lives at sea. A caring pedestrian saves someone who was about to fall over. How does Jesus save us and why the title Saviour?

In Matthew chapter 1, an angel of the Lord tells Joseph to name the child Jesus, 'because he will save his people from their sins.' The name 'Jesus,' is lovely. It brings together the name of God and the idea of being saved. 'Jesus' means 'God saves' or 'God is salvation'. In Hebrew it means salvation. He saves us from our sins.

That does sound religious but when we think of all that goes wrong with the world and how destructive humanity often seems to be to itself and to the planet, we can see that we need someone to change things for the better. Our bodies decay. Death comes to all. The Bible calls death an 'enemy' and it really feels like that since it robs us of our loved ones and creates fear. It is somehow the result of sin and so much decay. It is creation gone wrong and we need someone to put it right. The prophet Isaiah in the Old Testament says that a light has dawned on those living in the land of the shadow of death. Someone has come to put things right.

Jesus is our Saviour. He saves, or rescues us from ourselves and even from death. His forgiving and cleansing love from the cross and the new life he gives through his resurrection, rescues us in every way from destroying ourselves, each other and from death. His resurrection is the beginning of a New Creation. Everything will be put right. Our work here on earth now is to co-work with God in making the world a more loving, forgiving place, doing good, helping the disadvantaged and standing for justice.

> Lord, my Saviour. Thank you for saving me.
> Thank you for the new heaven and new
> earth which you give.

A FINAL THOUGHT—IS THERE ANY MEANING IN MY SUFFERING?

Read some verses from Psalm 22:

> *My God, my God, why have you forsaken me? Why are you so far from saving me, so far from the words of my groaning?*
>
> *O my God, I cry out by day, but you do not answer, by night, and am not silent.*
>
> *Do not be far from me, for trouble is near and there is no-one to help.*
>
> *I am poured out like water, and all my bones are out of joint. My heart is turned to wax; it has melted away within me.*
>
> *My strength is dried up like a potsherd, and my tongue sticks to the roof of my mouth; you lay me in the dust of death.*
>
> *I can count all my bones; people stare and glare over me.*
>
> *They divide my garments among them and cast lots for my clothing.*

This is about complete and utter hopelessness, complete dereliction. The person feels completely abandoned. God, have you forgotten me? Jesus used the first verse of this psalm when he hung on the cross. See how this psalm seems to speak of Jesus' crucifixion.

In deep depression it is very hard to have faith. God seems to have gone, there is just empty space where he was. It seems we lay in the dust of death.

In our dark suffering times, in the hopeless abandonment, we are actually suffering as Jesus suffered. We are sharing in his sufferings.

The world threw its worst at Jesus and we too are experiencing something of the worst the world throws out. We are struggling with some of the worst, just as Jesus struggled with it. We are sharing in the battle.

I like the feeling of being close to Jesus and standing alongside him in the heat of the battle. As he gets wounded, I expect nothing less. It really hurts, but it is good to serve alongside him and to feel he counts me worthy to share in this battle with him. I am on his winning side and one day we will sit enjoying the victory.

> Lord, you felt abandoned by God on the cross. I feel abandoned too. I suffer like you did. I don't understand it yet, but I put my hope in you even though I don't feel you there. As the cross led to resurrection, lead me please out of this illness and into new life. You did something wonderful for everyone out of your suffering. Please do something useful with mine.

Keep hope alive, keep going, well done.

If you are in hospital or perhaps in detention, talk to the chaplain.

If no one around you understands, talk to the local vicar. You may not be used to church people, but they tend on the whole to be kind and friendly. Church leaders are there for you too.

God be with you.

www.ingramcontent.com/pod-product-compliance
Lightning Source LLC
Chambersburg PA
CBHW071253070526
44583CB00017B/2445